How to Draw
Vermont's
Sights and Symbols

Stephanie True Peters

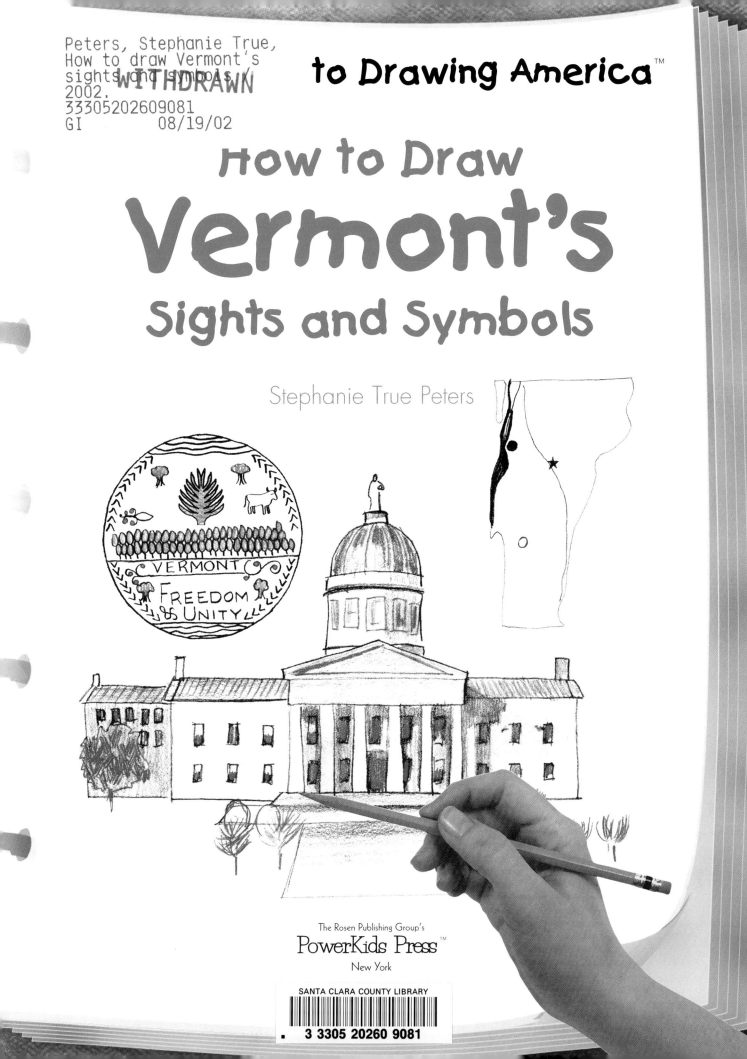

The Rosen Publishing Group's
PowerKids Press™
New York

Published in 2002 by The Rosen Publishing Group, Inc.
29 East 21st Street, New York, NY 10010

First Edition

Editor: Jannell Khu
Book Design: Kim Sonsky
Layout Design: Colin Dizengoff

Illustration Credits: Laura Murawski
Photo Credits: p. 7 © CORBIS; pp. 8–9 courtesy of Eleanor V. Mac Nicoll; pp. 12, 14 © One Mile Up, Incorporated; p. 16 © Buddy Mays/CORBIS; p. 18 © Lynda Richardson/CORBIS; p. 20 © Robert Estall/CORBIS; p. 22 © Kit Houghton Photography/CORBIS; p. 24 © Index Stock; p. 26 © Lee Snider; Lee Snider/CORBIS; p. 28 © Joseph Sohm; ChromoSohm, Inc./CORBIS.

Peters, Stephanie True, 1965–
How to draw Vermont's sights and symbols / Stephanie True Peters.
p. cm. — (A kid's guide to drawing America)
Includes index.
Summary: This book explains how to draw some of Vermont's sights and symbols, including the state seal, the official flower, and the Ethan Allen homestead.
   ISBN 0-8239-6102-8
1. Emblems, State—Vermont—Juvenile literature 2. Vermont—In art—Juvenile literature 3. Drawing—Technique—Juvenile literature   [1. Emblems, State—Vermont 2. Vermont 3. Drawing—Technique]
I. Title II. Series
   743'.8'99743—dc21

Manufactured in the
United States of America

CONTENTS

1	Let's Draw Vermont	4
2	The Green Mountain State	6
3	Artist in Vermont	8
4	Map of Vermont	10
5	The State Seal	12
6	The State Flag	14
7	The Red Clover	16
8	The Hermit Thrush	18
9	The Sugar Maple	20
10	The Morgan Horse	22
11	The Ethan Allen Homestead	24
12	Bennington Battle Monument	26
13	Vermont's Capitol	28
	Vermont State Facts	30
	Glossary	31
	Index	32
	Web Sites	32

Let's Draw Vermont

When you think of Vermont, you may think of maple syrup, cows, and beautiful fall foliage. Vermont is a top producer of milk and dairy products. Vermont is the home of one especially famous dairy product. In 1978, Ben Cohen and Jerry Greenfield decided to open their business in Vermont. That business was Ben & Jerry's ice cream. Today their rich ice cream is famous and is sold worldwide. Visitors to the Ben & Jerry's plant, located north of Waterbury, can see how ice cream is made and can sample free ice cream!

Fall is Vermont's most popular tourist season. When the leaves of the sugar maples and the other trees change color, people travel to Vermont from around the world to see nature's spectacular show. Fall is also when Vermont's apple crop is ready to harvest. Visitors can pick the fruit from any one of the state's 4,000 acres (1,619 ha) of apple orchards. They can also watch how apple cider is made and can buy gallons of the tart, sweet drink to enjoy at home. Vermont apple orchards produce more than 1 million bushels (35,239 kl) of apples annually!

Barre, Vermont, calls itself the Granite Center of the World. In the late 1800s, it was a leading producer of granite. Artisans from around the world came to Barre to cut and to carve the granite into beautiful works of art. Granite is still quarried in Barre, and many beautiful examples of stonework can be seen there. This book will show you how to draw some of Vermont's sights and symbols. Instructions help you through each step. New steps are shown in red. The list below shows some of the shapes you will draw. You will need the following supplies to draw Vermont's sights and symbols:

- A sketch pad
- An eraser
- A number 2 pencil
- A pencil sharpener

These are some of the shapes and drawing terms you need to know to draw Vermont's sights and symbols:

3-D box

Almond shape

Horizontal line

Oval

Rectangle

Shading

Squiggle

Teardrop

Vertical line

Wavy line

The Green Mountain State

The name Vermont comes from the French words *vert*, which means "green," and *mont*, which means "mountain." According to one story, clergyman Samuel Peters first used these words to describe the area in 1761. Mountains can be seen from nearly every place in this small state. It's not surprising that Vermont's nickname is the Green Mountain State!

Several important politicians are native to Vermont. Stephen A. Douglas (1813–1861) was born near Brandon, Vermont. He is best known for a series of debates with future president Abraham Lincoln during the 1858 Illinois senate race. Two vice presidents were also born in Vermont. Chester A. Arthur (1829–1886) was born in Fairfield, Vermont. He became vice president when President James A. Garfield was assassinated. Calvin Coolidge (1872–1933), was also vice president before he became president. He became president when Warren G. Harding died during his term. Coolidge was born in Plymouth, Vermont, on the fourth of July.

Two years after his famous debates, Senator Stephen A. Douglas was the Democratic nominee for president. He lost the election to Abraham Lincoln.

Artist in Vermont

Eleanor Mac Nicoll was born in New Jersey in 1927. She loved to paint and to draw when she was only a preschooler. That love has stayed with her all her life. She studied art at Mary Washington College in Virginia.

Eleanor Mac Nicoll

Eleanor lived in Vermont for many years. The beauty of Vermont and its neighboring New England states inspires her to paint. Once a young boy watched her paint on the rocky shores in Maine. Eleanor pointed out to the boy that the rocks seemed to be a dull gray until you looked closely. Then you could see other colors, like pink, purple, and blue. Later that same day she overheard the boy asking his friends to look for the colors in the rocks! Eleanor painted *Road*

Mac Nicoll used pencil to sketch this farmhouse in 1997. She named it *New England House*.

Past Vermont Farmhouse in the Fall to give to a friend who moved from Vermont to Connecticut. The painting captures the many elements for which Vermont is famous. It was painted during Vermont's most beautiful season. Eleanor painted the bright autumn leaves that stand out against a clear blue sky, dotted with white clouds. Vermont is known for its many red barns and quiet little dirt roads lined with trees. Eleanor said, "I always have hope and look for the brightness at the end of the road, as seen in the painting."

Eleanor Mac Nicoll painted *Road Past Vermont Farmhouse in the Fall* in 1999. It was done in watercolor and measures 30" x 21" (76 cm x 53 cm). Eleanor said, "When painting, I like to choose subjects that are beautiful and entertaining—with some interesting story to tell."

Map of Vermont

Map of the Continental United States

Vermont can be divided into four regions. In the northwest corner is the Champlain Valley. This area is also called the Vermont Lowlands. The Champlain Valley is flat with rich soil and has the state's best farmland. The Northeast Highlands, or Northeast Kingdom, has dense forests with many animals. This area is sparsely populated with people. The Northeast Highlands has many forests and is called logging country. South of this area are the Eastern Foothills. Dairy farms and apple orchards are found here. The mountain regions are broken into two chains, the Taconic Range and the Green Mountains. The Taconic Range is in the southwest. The Green Mountains are in the middle of the state.

1

Draw the shape above. It is made with six connected lines.

2

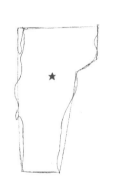

To shape Vermont, copy the red lines as shown above. Notice that the top and the bottom part of the state remain mostly straight. Draw a five-pointed star for the state capital, Montpelier. Erase extra lines.

3

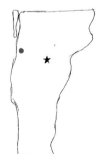

Draw a black circle toward the top left. This is the city of Burlington.

4

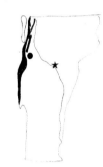

Draw lines that run along the upper left side of the state. Shade in the lines. This is Lake Champlain.

5

Great! Next draw a wavy line from the upper left portion of the state down to the lower right. You just drew White River.

6

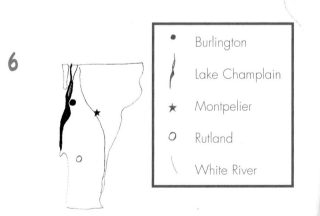

•	Burlington
⌠	Lake Champlain
★	Montpelier
O	Rutland
\	White River

Draw a circle toward the bottom of the state. This is the city of Rutland. You can also draw the map key if you like.

11

The State Seal

Vermont's state seal was adopted in 1779. The original design was changed four times between 1821 and 1898. Then in 1937, the Vermont legislature voted to reproduce and to adopt the original seal, which is the seal used today. In the middle of the seal is a pine tree with 14 branches. Thirteen of the branches represent the original 13 colonies. Vermont is the fourteenth branch, because it was the fourteenth state to be admitted into the Union. The lines at the top of the seal stand for the sky. The lines at the bottom stand for water. Across the middle of the seal is a row of tree-covered hills. Four bundles of wheat and a cow represent Vermont's agriculture.

Written in the bottom half of the seal is Vermont's motto, "Vermont, Freedom & Unity".

1

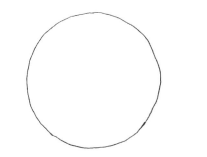

Draw a circle. Make sure it is large enough to fit in all the images you will draw.

2

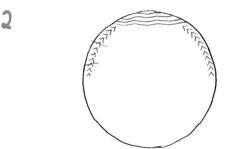

Toward the top center, draw four wavy lines. On either side of the circle, draw 11 small shapes that look like upside-down Vs.

3

Draw a horizontal line. On the bottom of the circle, draw four wavy lines. On either side of the circle, draw 10 small shapes that look like Vs.

4

Draw four bundles of wheat. Two go above the horizontal line and two go below.

5

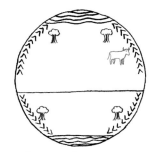

For the cow, draw a basic rectangle for the body and a triangle for the head. Then add shapes for the legs, the tail, and the horns. Erase extra lines for the cow.

6

Draw the tree in the center. The tree should have 14 branches. For the small rows of trees, draw ovals. You don't have to draw the exact amount that you see.

7

Draw the shape to the left of the tree. Write the word "VERMONT" and underline it. Draw the design on either side. Now write "FREEDOM & UNITY" beneath it.

8

Shade, and you're done!

13

The State Flag

Vermont adopted its state flag in 1923. The seal that is on the flag is the version that Vermont adopted in 1821. This seal is centered on a field of blue. It shows a scene with a single, large pine tree, a cow, and three bundles of wheat. These represent Vermont's lumber, dairy, and farming industries. In the background are more pine trees and mountains. These represent Vermont's landscape. Surrounding the scene is a border of gold. Above the coat of arms is a stag's head, which stands for Vermont's wildlife. Written below the coat of arms is Vermont's motto, "Vermont, Freedom & Unity", on a banner of red. Pine boughs frame half of the coat of arms.

1

Draw a rectangle. Lightly draw a vertical and a horizontal line in the middle of the rectangle. These lines will help you in the next steps.

2

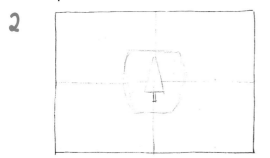

Lightly draw a shield in the center of the rectangle. Draw the pine tree.

3

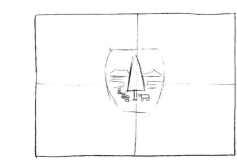

Draw the mountains behind the tree. Add lines for the land. Draw three mushroom shapes for the bundles of wheat. Draw the cow to the right of the tree.

4

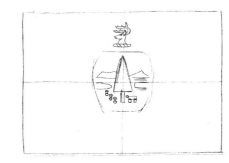

Draw the stag's head above the shield. Study the stag before you start.

5

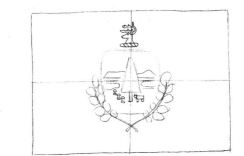

Great job! Now draw the decorative leaf design on either side of the shield.

6

Draw the ribbon border on the bottom of the shield. It needs to be large enough to write in some words later on.

7

Draw the decorative design all around the shield.

8

Write "FREEDOM" on the left side of the ribbon. Write "VERMONT" in the middle. Finally, write "UNITY" on the right side of the ribbon. Shade, and you're done.

15

The Red Clover

Vermont adopted the red clover as its state flower in 1894. The daisy, the mayflower, and the arbutus were also considered. Those who supported the red clover pointed out that it was an important plant for the state's dairy industry. Cows like to eat red clover. Red clover is good for cows, because it is rich in vitamins A and E. In addition red clover puts nitrogen back into the soil. Nitrogen is a mineral. Plants grow better in nitrogen-rich soil. Farmers who want to put nitrogen back into the soil naturally will often seed their fields with red clover in between crops. People have used the red clover as a natural cure for years. It is said to help coughs, skin rashes, bug bites, and stings. Some people believe it may even help cure cancer!

1

Draw an oval. Draw two long, vertical, parallel lines that extend from the oval. This is the stem.

2

Begin to draw the little pointed petals. Notice that some are oval shaped and others are shaped like bananas!

3

Continue to draw the petals. Don't worry about making them perfect. Just focus on the general shapes. Notice that the bottom petals near the stem are large.

4

Shade in the drawing by turning your pencil on its side and lightly stroking the paper. Shade the lighter areas first, then go back and shade the darker areas. Have fun!

The Hermit Thrush

The hermit thrush almost wasn't chosen as Vermont's state bird. The hermit thrush migrates south in the winter and returns to Vermont in the spring. Some people felt that their state bird should live in Vermont year-round. They wanted the chickadee or the blue jay instead. Both of these birds make their homes in Vermont all year. However, the hermit thrush is the only bird found in all of Vermont's 14 counties. It became Vermont's official state bird on June 1, 1941.

The hermit thrush lives close to the ground. It builds its nest in the low branches of shrubs or trees and lays light blue eggs. When the baby birds are strong enough, they hop along the ground, following behind their mother for many days before they learn to fly.

1

For the bird's body, draw an oval that angles slightly toward the left. Draw a smaller, egg-shaped oval on top of the first one. This is the head.

2

Connect the two ovals together. Draw the outline of the wings and the tail. Draw a small triangle for the beak. Erase extra lines.

3

Draw the branch at a downward angle from left to right. Next draw the bird's skinny legs and its claws.

4

Draw a circle for the eye. Add a line in the middle of the beak. Lightly sketch in the patterns and the details on the feathers.

5

Shade your bird, and you're done!

The Sugar Maple

The sugar maple became Vermont's state tree in 1929. Maple syrup and other maple products are made from the sap of the sugar maple. Sap is liquid that comes out of trees. To get the sap,

special spouts, called spiles, are hammered into the sugar maples in late winter. The sap drips into buckets hung beneath the spiles or flows along plastic tubing into a bin. When enough sap is collected, it is carefully boiled down. Forty gallons (151 l) of sap are needed to make 1 gallon (4 l) of syrup! Sugar-on-snow is a popular Vermont treat. To make it, maple syrup is poured on fresh, clean snow. The snow hardens the syrup into delicious candy! In the fall, the sugar maple's leaves turn beautiful shades of red, yellow, and orange.

1

Draw two vertical lines that come to a point at the top. This is the trunk. Notice that the lines are not perfectly straight.

2

First lightly draw a big cloud shape over the tree. This will be the area where the leaves will be. Next turn your pencil on its side and lightly shade the area of the leaves. You can shade some areas darker than other areas.

3

Look at the drawing shown in this step, and shape the tree by erasing some of the cloud area you drew in step 2. Next press the tip of your pencil to shade little dark patches all over the tree's leaf area. Don't worry about making it perfect. You're just trying to get the general look of the tree.

4

Fill in the tree's trunk. You're almost done. Now all you have to do is define the tree's branches. Good job!

The Morgan Horse

Vermont adopted the Morgan horse as its state animal on March 23, 1961. Less than 200 years earlier, this breed of horse did not exist! A colt named Figure was born in Massachusetts in 1789. When Figure's owner and breeder, Justin Morgan, moved from Massachusetts to Vermont, he took Figure with him. Figure was stronger, faster, and worked harder than any other horse the people of Vermont had ever seen. They all wanted a horse just like "Morgan's horse." Figure's offspring were just as strong, fast, and hardworking as he was. Today any horse descended from Figure is known as a Morgan horse. His descendants carried Vermont's cavalry into battle during the Civil War (1861–1865).

1

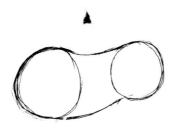

First draw a circle on the left side of your paper. Add a slightly smaller circle on the right. Next connect the two circles. This will be the basic shape of the horse's body.

2

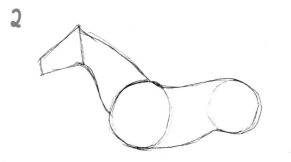

Draw two lines that extend from the left circle. This is the neck. For the head, draw four lines that make up the angled shape.

3

Erase extra lines. For the front leg, draw two straight vertical lines. Draw the shape of the hoof. To draw the hind leg, draw the lines at an angle.

4

Draw in the details of the hooves at the bottom of the legs. Add a vertical line in the front legs. Then draw a line for the hind leg. Now the horse looks like it has four legs! Draw in the nose, the eye, and the ears. Draw the tail.

5

Slowly shade the drawing by turning your pencil on its side and lightly stroking the paper. Be patient!

The Ethan Allen Homestead

Ethan Allen (1738–1789) is an important figure in Vermont's history. Before Vermont became a state, New Hampshire and New York fought over its land. Allen wanted Vermont to be an independent state. He and a band of men called the Green Mountain Boys tried to drive the New Yorkers out of Vermont. During the American Revolution, Allen led this same band on a raid on Fort Ticonderoga. His victory there won Allen and his men a place in history. The Ethan Allen Homestead is in Burlington, Vermont. On this historic site is a reconstruction of Allen's last home and a visitor's center with a store. Volunteers show visitors what life was like in the 1700s.

1

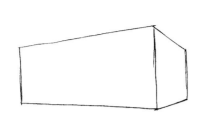

Draw a 3-D rectangle. This shape is drawn with seven lines. Here's a tip. Draw the horizontal lines at slight angles.

2

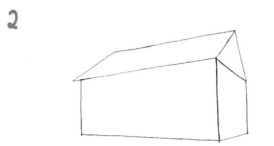

Draw a 3-D triangle on top of the rectangle. This is the roof.

3

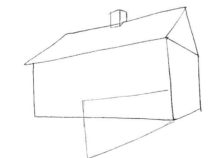

Draw the chimney on top of the roof. Next draw three lines that extend from the house. This will be the woodpile stand.

4

Erase the horizontal line under the triangle shape. Draw rectangles for the windows. Add the door on the front of the house.

5

Add detail to the woodpile stand. Fill the stand with fire logs. First draw small circles. Next draw lines from the upper circles and the side circles as shown.

6

Add details to the front windows. Next shade the house. Make the roof light and the front of the house a little darker. Draw horizontal lines across the front of the house. You're done!

Bennington Battle Monument

The Battle of Bennington was fought during the American Revolution. A British general named John Burgoyne wanted to raid American storehouses in Bennington, Vermont. His troops made it as far as a hill in New York, 5 miles (8 km) from Bennington. There, on August 16, 1777, they were met by American troops. Some of these Americans were the Green Mountain Boys. They were led by a man named Seth Warner. The two sides fought all day. In the end, the Americans won and saved the supplies! A monument to the Battle of Bennington stands in Bennington. The granite tower stands 306 feet (93 m) tall. In front of the monument is a statue of Seth Warner. He stands guard over the site where an arsenal once stood.

1

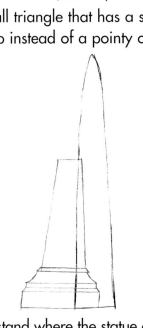

Draw a tall triangle that has a slightly curved top instead of a pointy one.

2

Draw the stand where the statue of Seth Warner will stand. First draw several stacked rectangles for the base. Then add the tall, rectangular block of stone above the base.

3

Next draw the top part of the stand. First study the shapes, then draw one line at a time.

4

Draw the statue of Seth Warner. Draw his head first. Next draw his body, his legs, and his arms. His right arm is folded against his chest. Finally, draw a line for his sword. Add details to the triangle shape behind Warner.

5

Erase extra lines. Shade your drawing, and you're done!

27

Vermont's Capitol

Montpelier became Vermont's capital city in 1805. The first statehouse was a wooden structure finished in 1808. Over time, the building started to fall apart. When the legislature outgrew it, it was torn down. A second statehouse was completed in 1838. It was made of granite from Barre, Vermont. The inside of this building was destroyed by fire in January 1857. Two and one-half years later, the third and final statehouse was finished. Vermont's capitol building is one of the most beautiful capitols in the nation. It stands against the backdrop of Vermont's green, wooded hills. The building features a gold dome. A wooden statue of Ceres, the Roman goddess of agriculture, stands on top of the dome.

1

Draw a horizontal rectangle. On the left side, draw a square that is slightly shorter than the rectangle.

2

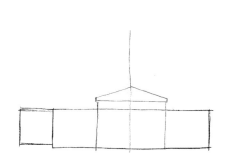

Draw another rectangle in the middle of the long rectangle. Next draw a triangular roof on top of it. Add a long vertical line. It should cut through the middle part of the roof and go down to the bottom.

3

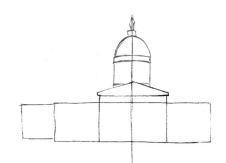

Draw a smaller rectangle on top of the triangle. Draw two slightly curved lines above that. Draw a half circle on top. This is the dome. Draw the little rectangle and the figure on the top.

4

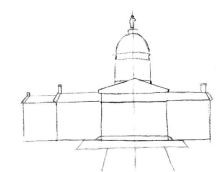

Draw horizontal lines above the rectangles. This is the roof. Draw little angled lines and boxes. Next let's draw the stairs. Draw the lines that extend from the building as shown. Erase extra lines.

5

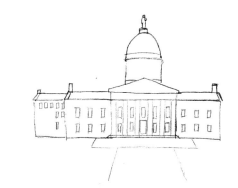

Draw little rectangles for the windows. Draw six columns underneath the triangle.

6

Draw in the trees in front of the building. Shade your drawing gradually, and add detail to the dome. Really nice work!

Vermont State Facts

Statehood	March 4, 1791, 14th state
Area	9,615 square miles (24,903 sq km)
Population	591,000
Capital	Montpelier, population, 7,900
Most Populated City	Burlington, population, 39,000
Industries	Electronic equipment, printing and publishing, paper products, tourism
Agriculture	Dairy products, apples, maple products, cattle, hay
Animal	
Nickname	The Green Mountain State
Motto	Vermont, Freedom & Unity
Precious Stone	Grossular garnet
Rocks	Granite, marble, slate
Insect	Honeybee
Animal	Morgan horse
Bird	Hermit thrush
Flower	Red clover
Tree	Sugar maple
Amphibian	Northern leopard frog
Fossil	White whale

Glossary

American Revolution (uh-MER-uh-ken reh-vuh-LOO-shun) Battles that soldiers from the colonies fought against England for freedom.

arsenal (AR-sih-nuhl) A storehouse of weapons.

artisans (AR-tih-zenz) A term for craftsmen or a mechanics. People with a type of job that usually involves manual labor and the production or the repair of material items.

assassinated (uh-SA-sin-ayt-ed) To have murdered an important or famous person.

cavalry (KA-vul-ree) The part of an army that rides horses.

clergyman (KLUR-jee-muhn) A minister, a priest, or a rabbi.

debates (duh-BAYTZ) Discussions between two people where each person takes a different position on a selected topic.

descended (dih-SEN-ded) Born of a certain family or group.

foliage (FOH-lee-ihj) Leaves, flowers, or branches of plants and trees.

granite (GRA-niht) Melted rock that cooled and hardened beneath Earth's surface.

legislature (LEH-jihs-lay-cher) A body of people that has the power to make or pass laws.

logging (LAHG-ing) The act or business of cutting down trees.

migrates (MY-grayts) Moves from one place to another.

mineral (MIH-neh-rul) A substance, such as gold or silver, that is found in the earth and that is not a plant or an animal.

quarried (KWOR-eed) Dug out, mined.

reconstruction (ree-kahn-STRUHK-shun) To rebuild.

Index

A
Allen, Ethan, 24
American Revolution,
       24, 26

B
Ben & Jerry's, 4
Bennington Battle
       Monument, 26
Burlington, VT, 24

C
capitol, 28
Champlain Valley, 10
Civil War, 22
cow(s), 4, 12, 14,
       16

E
Ethan Allen
       Homestead, 24

G
granite, 5, 26
Green Mountain Boys,
       24, 26

M
Mac Nicoll, Eleanor,
       8–9
Montpelier, 28
Morgan horse, 22

P
Peters, Samuel, 6

S
state bird, 18
state flag, 14
state flower, 16
state seal, 12
sugar maple, 20
syrup, 4, 20

Web Sites

To learn more about Vermont, check out these Web sites:
www.50states.com/vermont.htm
www.geobop.com/World/NA/US/VT
www.virtualvermont.com